Some Days, Here

From Pebble
to Ripple

TRICIA DE JESUS-GUTIERREZ

authorHOUSE®

AuthorHouse™
1663 Liberty Drive
Bloomington, IN 47403
www.authorhouse.com
Phone: 1 (800) 839-8640

Published by AuthorHouse 02/07/2017

ISBN: 978-1-5246-6943-0 (sc)
ISBN: 978-1-5246-6942-3 (e)

Print information available on the last page.

Contents

"To the company
of enlightened conversation
and good, strong coffee."

FOREWORD

Native & Alien

Born to a Navy man and a housewife who immigrated from the simplified beauties of slow moving farm life in the Philippines to the bustle of a new life in the States, eventually settling down in a little Bay Area town; Tricia De Jesus-Gutierrez found herself ever native and alien to this world among worlds, in thought and actuality. The clang and clamor of a culture both foreign and first person with its ores, slag, and ash, turn the corners of her thoughts, color the iris and follicle, imbue her experiences as much as that of her equally present American culture and its molten admixture. Aren't we all, no matter if our point of origin is singular or dual, native and alien? The author understands this peculiar pathos in which we belong, by no choice of our own, to this whirling ball of confounding dust and water and yet, do not belong at all. She also registers with great depth and clarity how, paradoxically, the people and things we've drawn in and collected around us like tides which will inevitably recede, are both native to us by laws of attraction and settlement, and alien in their own autonomous state and unavoidable migration - it is all transient after all.

I discovered the distinct privilege of coming to know Tricia in 2013. We met across time zones in a writers group where we all started out like heavily veiled brides exposing only our words at first and coming to know each other through the shared brokenness and love within those lines. Eventually this swelled and spilled out into life outside of the group and I learned of her deep affinity for her animals, her altruistic heart, and the true vehemence of her love for literature and letter writing. Tricia is a very private soul, but she has chosen to bare herself on these pages that we might come lean in close to her sometimes whisper, sometimes scream, sometimes growl. You will not find her easy for nothing worthwhile ever comes that way, she is not a fluency curling off the tongue and you are privileged that this is so. You will, instead, find her lain beneath rich wording and between stout lines, opaque and dusky as memory, yet vibrant and sanguine as the coppery vermillion sustaining life.

Tricia wields a spellbinding grasp of language in "Some Days, Here". The intrinsic probity of her poetic voice compels surrender to its offering. Even in those places where she is esoteric or ambiguous, the reader can glean layered meaning and take small bites of the author's inception. She takes us on a journey from innocence to loss through her childhood memories and conditioned misconceptions of beauty, sense of self, to loves found and misplaced, melding the vibrancy of her aches with the richness of her quiver of beauties. Belonging and not belonging, the innate quest for freedom, love, and acceptance, but also justice, needle themselves in as central threads in these poems. The poems are aware, however, of their own idealism at times, in an ever out of kilter existence and often speak in ironies.

Innocence is the first chapter of this book and the shortest, alluding to the fact that we are disavowed of our illusions and naiveties, even some of our beauty and purities early on. The lessons of life's blows come swift and hard, but we are revived by the rich love that surrounds us always. Always are we surrounded by love. Her words are spoken from a tongue of bone your teeth must work to get to the marrow of but once there, you taste her openness, for this marrow offers up a confession. There is a slight nudge from her body to yours into the direction of her thoughts and the self is discovered within her rare heart, its cracks where we wedge our own, its rooms left ready for visitors.

Tricia explores perceived beauty and the arcing flaw of saudade playing against each other. This holds strong sub-textual inference to the author herself feeling less than beautiful, or not so factored in a reality that does not hold her aesthetic at highest regard. The greater implication here is the dissolving of self-worth when thrust against the measuring stick of a standard not intended. We've all experienced this on some level. We find also among these pages the bruises of abuse, some ochred due to the mercy of time and others a fresh carmine, from the burden and guttural expulsions of religiosity's weight on the conscience.

The author draws us closely into her interior with the sense of meaninglessness in the search for oneself in other bodies and other things. Never told that she can grow a garden, even if just within herself, even if no one else knew about it. She is a flowering thing, left to find her own water much too often while streams run in ignorance, to some elsewhere. She was never told that boys are not raised to tend to flowers but harvest them, then prepare for the next growing season.

In this life to which we are native and alien, there is a want to believe that in all its facets love's intentions are good, a want for the repositioning of air, for some method of alteration, as one throws themselves into the mesh of inevitable failures, losses, and pain. In all of this, the suffering, the cleaving and falling away, the searching, as the writer, herself asserts "it appears love has everything to do with it…don't make us bullied fools for nothing".

- Elle Arra
February 2017

I. Innocence

Anne Marie

Cherished friendships become
lodged into the archives of our fond
consciousness

But what of the forgotten friend?
A wayward wind through our life,
settling for an instance, never
so much as a demarcation
on our story, before slipping through
the cracks of our memory?

I will stand completely still,
dig deeply into neglected crevices,
call out to that little girl
who seems to have melted
into time itself.

I cannot say for sure
but maybe her name was Anne Marie.

Our family moved in next to hers
the summer I was five years old.

What returns to me about her
were her impossibly rosy cheeks,
her long, corn silk blonde hair
darker at the roots.

I hardly remember seeing her daddy
at home, except for blurry glimpses
of a burly, furry bear of a man, her
diminutive mother not an outright beauty
but a Japanese novelty among white
bread military wives.

Anne Marie beguiled me daily,
impish eyes and ever present tinkling
laughter, the magic of her effervescent
presence, gaiety without guile
flitting through the sunset lit
dandelion fluff of our youth
and innocence.

I did not know at that
tender period what being
biracial even meant, much as I
had not a clue what my own dark eyes
and brown skin may have looked like
to untried eyes.

All I knew on those long
summer days, were the important truths any
kindergartner needed to know: tadpoles
become frogs, crab apples were a sour delight
and Anne Marie was the most beautiful creature
in the whole wide world.

second recess

we played
  in the sandbox
skinned knees
and pigtails loose
we were explorers
sporks were shovels
and red clay was gold
I think we were
digging
   all the way
   to Kathmandu
or maybe Timbuktu
  we would decide
once we got there
fifth graders ruled
the playground
we would get
pushed out
of the sandbox
   more often
   than not
by bullies who seemed
like ogres and giants
  on
   our
lilliputian
   island.

Nineteen-Seventy-Six

Where the hand is placed
a pendulous swing
beneath trusting eyes
and conversation

Beer after beer
at a subtle coaxing
should not mix well
with pigtails
and patent leather
Mary-Janes

Where the hand is placed
a thunderous clap
beneath meticulously ironed lace
upon bewildered skin

Kiss after kiss
against terrified protestation
should not mix well
with pigtails
and patent leather
Mary-Janes

A Mary Cherry

Our Lord's
disapproval
factored heavily
but it was still Mother
Superior's face
superimposed
alongside *Tiya*
Lucia's worried brow
fretting, pinching, tucking,
my maidenhood
at stake on
a banana seat bike.
All this ran
before my eyes
before your concentrating
nervous visage
sweat like fascinating
beads suspended above mine
staring hard
to maintain my composure
thinking about everything
anything else
to defuse my fear

to dilute my embarrassment
and inept caresses
as you spear
miss
and--bull's-eye!
a moment's
pinpoint pain
a cherry
deconstructed
a culmination
or genesis
to a lifetime worth
of Catholic
schoolgirl guilt.

Berkeley Nights

You lead me through
the elder trees
I followed
no fear
no questions
asked

Slight rancid taste
upon my lips
hint of days
spent working;
chain smoking
on self-imposed breaks
nights hustling,
scrabbling
for gigs, for fortune,
for home

I was never home
but I was comfort
you were never solace
but danger
I craved you
an exciting
departure

I glimpse
that life now
startling sips
once desperate
and familiar
now alien
as I meander
among the elders.

II. Creatures

For Love of Cute Carnivores

Once live and standing
vermilion slab offering
I truly love you.

Pseudo-Jacobsonizing

Poised in textbook
distaste, nose a perfect
pug-like crease, lips pulled
back, ineffective predator
all front teeth bared.
Not quite serpentine or
felinesque in my stance,
the grimace, nonetheless
does its trick: I can smell you,
oily, metallic, beneath the clean,
your deceitful malodour.

toy dilemma

head tilts quizzically
tail is in full *rat-tat-tat*
serious topic
squeaky bone? or squeaky chicken?
beautiful hazel eyes
momentarily
worried with making
the right decision

Sucker for the Oddities
(Can We Keep It?)

Are you ever struck with an unbidden
desire to change up something
in the monotony of your life?
For example: did you
one day decide you would walk
the long way to work just for the sake
of doing something different?
Have you ever done just that?
You know? Take a walk deep in thought
and imagined for a split second
you were being observed
silently by giant lime-green orbs?
Did you--more feel than hear-- velvet pats
upon the ground behind you
only to look back rapidly nervously
and find it's still you and your musings?
Would you begin to walk with more purpose?
Run? Hide and peep out?
Try to catch a minute-sized glimpse
of this fleet fur-booted phantom? Do you
suppose curiosity will get the better of you
and you will opt to sit and wait?
Maybe even coo alluring cute nonsense?
Will it be "here kitty kitty?"
or "who's a good little boy?"

What was your reaction
when a substantial
hooked paw
materialized
from thin air?
those imagined
reptilian eyes
now reality?
followed by
a poofed
and spiked
ebony tail?

Would you scream then?
In terror?
In delight?

Pot Pie & Legs (Chicken Everything, Kittens & Table Manners)

We should have had a clue
the day my son pet-sat the furballs
and happily reported back to us
at the end of the day, "My favourite
is Cheeseburger Kitten." We should have
known this was not a millennial's
reference to a popular meme.

We should have suspected
the day we adopted her, on the trip
back home, when we stopped
for Jack-in-the-Box, that her cries
were not only mewling borne
of fright, but also possibly hunger
(hunger for a sourdough patty melt).

We swear to the foodie spirits
we had not a clue. Her curiosity was not
unusual, if anything, tipping the scale
to cliche. We swear she only ever sniffed
the air, tasted the essence of delectable
meats on her tongue, before going about
her normal kitten business.

That is
That was

until we adopted her baby sister
and as a tandem they plied their wily trade.
One sister, all claws and fluff and charm,
floofed tortoiseshell glove in the steaming
pot pie, the elder, all tabby wiry and stealth
and grace

      making off
         with a chicken leg
            twice
               her size.

Amor de Mi Vida

Silken Milk
and Soft Tiger Boy
your startling orbs
are my eternity
melting twin
summer sunsets
I am dazzled
every
single
time

Vulnerable
in the thrall
of your never-
waning charm
of your steady
regard.

My love
and being
rise and set
with you.

Amusements

I, cat
a black shadow
and a sudden
thought:
I shall pounce
on you
mightily
the passing
weight of a feather
or a kiss

You will never
know what
came to pass.

III. LOVE & LUST

dame noir

you carmine lipped minx
you have flip-flopped orbit
turn the moon my way

Look at Me

Look
at me, No
look at me,
across a pregnant
divide, across
an unbreachable
chasm, and see

Is the shame
familiar? Is it
the skeleton
to your narrative,
a poem, asthmatic,
not epic, collecting,
building, an exhaustive,
repetitive refrain?

Look, see,
a blink reaction
remorse
but do not
commit me
to this farce.

each tidbit in six words

thoughts remain
benign
you at bay

brown eyes
are caramel
      i stumble

would
your lips
taste like
honeysuckle?

i saw you today
blue lace chemise

you hair
is sunburst
and chaos

it is infatuation
these things pass

Sugar & Spice

Peach pie
and honeyed-
cake peepers can flash
keylime at me

whenever they damn
well please. I won't
fret, I can't lie, I kind of
like the sass,

teasing
  trickle like
like fire
    whiskey
    droplets
      or straight-
              up
          moonshine
          gumption.

                    Sugar
                        and sting
                  mix it up
                      well.

Baby girl,

              I'll come back
              for seconds
              and then
              some.

Unfurling

my interest burgeoning
rings coquettishly toward you, perfect
tiny, crystal bells brushing the newness
of your milky petal face

my infatuation shadows
caution, its feather suede footfalls
whispering possibilities into the bouquet
of your impossible thistle hair

my desire courses red
erratic pulsations inside my ear, a roar
emerging from my veins, covert invasion
of your mocking bud, pistils sighing

my obsession laps
peripheral to your taunting aura, a sickening,
sugar-sticky reverberation, the sopping wet sounds
a worthy obstruction in your rosebud mouth.

Almost No, Isn't

(Hamilton's "Say No To This" had been an ear worm
at the time)

stay awhile

   wink part

troubles at bay
outside our door
the seedy hall
contains your harried
life for later
shamefaced
perusal

don't fret, lover
the walls
are thin
but they rejoice
in each reluctant
-addictive coupling

sigh

delve oft-stingy
comfort

your burdens
shed with your
shirt and your
scruples

the whole world
can change
tomorrow.

Dance Me, Fool

Curve
a blood-red
smile just right
at the corners
it no longer
comes easily
but old
vices
never die
away, they are
seduction, tucked
away, regressed,
until summoned
a reflex sneak
attack where
they assumed
there was no
more.
Just
look
at me
with
the right
gleam
in your
eyes

I do
not
make promises
to absolve
your sin
as I
stroke
your ego.

Sin Jar

Shelved sanctuary
three feet clearance above
my head, my shanty shame.

Slicked porcine
licks, repetition
upon my offer, broadcast
a tepid pale will
imprinted
upon my forehead:
Open
for business

No guilt sits staidly
at shot glass
bottom, no matter.
No room
in this far
removed, sanitized
life.

Once the Cynic, Always the Fool

What's love got to do with it
the chorus mimics the refrain
of every song ever written
in ode to lost causes

We pin precarious hope
and build upon ridiculed castles
I do not even know where we
leech the audacity for optimism
given nothing in this whole scenario
was a hearty yea to futures
painted in smarmy sunsets
and fluttering stomachs

At which point did we lose
the unsettling sensation
of being feed indiscretions
and outright lies?
Crusty, wizened reality
should really give pause
even through
the maw of the repeat offender
fashioned as its wont
to stick to the hard palate
of the stubbornly romantic.

It appears love
has everything to do with it
chorus, verse, and refrain
on endless loop it conquers
in every fathomable cliche
choke it down bravely
every opportunity we are afforded
don't make us bullied fools
for nothing.

Shokushu Amerika

"I am certain the belladonna
is to die for," smirking, winking,
"But only if there is more
where it came from."
This is the part in the B-movie
where he boldly slid
a single
tentacle
a vacuum receptor kiss
a temporarily permitted
appendage
upon her
outstretched
swan song.
One toggle
to emit a pleasure
response, one switch
to pretend a satiety
nowhere present.
A pedestal
upon which they divest
their skins, corporal lies
best left
at the threshold.

trainwreck/tanka (the deluded series)

I.
dive off the deep end
we'll wave you off at pool's edge
you don't see our frowns
your feet kicking at our shock
grown man don't need a life vest

II.
I will not opine
my silence roars my judgment
words would be wasted
upon your obstinate will
make your mistakes on your own

III.
beyond the world's eyes
who are we to say what goes
on behind closed doors? we know
perfection is subjective,
still, you are no less a fool.

IV.
I deduced how lust
became late night walks in heels
and significance
of diamond rings in boxes;
never the same neat ending.

V.
the time will never
be right, to address what we

are all thinking, the
the wretched Elephant will
not leave on her own.

VI.
today the face smiles
painted lips for your pleasure
just remember you
must perform the right function
to make the rest of her dance

IV. Life & Loss

Effigies

I waved
at effigies of you
as we sauntered past
smiling, sightless
dummies
of what our love
could have been

Of Morning Glories

Of the clank
of rusted pipes
of the pots
and pans
and pots
   and pans
a tide
of endless
monotony

Of coffee
that hums
both comfort
and inane
repetition
drip drip
   hisssss
day in
day out
faithful reprise

Of cushions
fashioned forts
and battlement
peek at
this world
at your
peril

Of princes
beneath
tightly closed
eyelids

Cheers to Your Worthy Ghosts

Slumber becomes
  suggestion, a hurried plea
as I barrel past, respite
for weary bones is not comfort
to a mind
   quibbling
    clawing
for answers

     to questions

not decisively framed
posed to no one
in particular

or anyone
who cares to listen

Doyouunderstand?
Do you see me standing
before you, right here
as you laugh
     and flit about
    chasing
     your noble
      ghosts?

Cicatrix

Ten years and some change,
I had two silver crescents--
one on my knee and one
on the back of my hand.
They were badges
of honour, large enough
to be distinct, small enough
to not be grotesque, somewhat
pretty in their lotteried shape.
Now they number in the hundreds
I would venture. I'd fancy them
stars, if I were hellbent on flattery.

How I Was Taught to Make Pico de Gallo

At a tender age, no not tender
but ripe, you are what you see,
what you dive into to, revel and steep,
when the presence that grounds
you is yanked out from underneath
a carpet at once verdant and humid
and loud and pungent and familiar,
familiar, what a jolt, for you thought
you would never comprehend it.
Now simmered
waist deep in an alien stew, a pot also at
once home and an adventure, you absorb its
tantalising flavours with every pore. First chop
the onions finely, to weep and purify, you reveal
an ache, nausea of homesick waves engulf, then
the chiles and cilantro, to embolden and renew,
you sample an ignored father-tongue, simultaneously
simple and unwieldy, you wing the eye and berry
the lip, the red, the final touch, tomatoes, ready and
bursting, to teach passion, compassion, camaraderie,
companionship, familia.

You now see, but you have always
seen in disapproving eyes, the otherness of this dish,
but what is foreign to those who will not care
to know, is a comforting pozole that warms you
all over, an affectionate mama who tends to not only
your stomach, but your questioning heart,
nonjudgmental siblings who took you in
and saved you from the cold
of separation and rejection.
Would you throw mama and her familia
and me out with yesterday's refuse?

What Once Was Mine

Comb of bone
scrapes through hair
keeps time with crazed
rocking. Haunting words
mouthed through parched lips
a repeated, lilting refrain.

SISTERTANKAS7

I.
bone was pulverized
in pathos and self-loathing.
i shed tears with you.
broken bodies mend slowly,
splintered hearts, unending pain.

II.
fair belle of the ball
dusky skin is second-class

i am adopted!

the world still spins despite me
second daughter lost in sulk

III.
you and i connect
where blood pools so easily
but trust is tricky
love makes the betrayal sting
even the pain imagined

IV.
i am just like you.
i am you, only other.
my words are your words,
you speak them and i repeat.
at times, i do the talking.

V.
Pepper was a pup.
This is where memory fails.
There were two and you drew them,
whimsy on a Sucrets tin.

VI.
I barely knew you,
city life imbued élan.
I still ate *tuyo*,
while your clique noshed on Shakey's
and my crimped hair was disgrace.

VII.
beaus past and present
none yet have been deemed worthy
no one breaks your heart
without rending mine to ash
stab one and the other screams

Just Right (Goldilocks and the Three Unequal Options)

Blessed are
the meek they shall
inherit the earth,
impressed upon tender
flesh and pink, open
bud mind, where can-do
can fast become reticence
and brashness was
reduced to cop shows
Maria Claras sometimes
watched on the television
but never admitted to for
fear of being branded unchaste.
"Ignorance is bliss" alighted
somewhat on the heels
of the former or even later still
a preemptive squash of teenaged
superiority, a subtle daily
reminder to know one's place, to
delight in one's limitations.
There is none among us
who are gods! Look at that fool
Icarus who flew to close to
the sun

the burn must
have felt
really nice
for a bit
but SPLAT!
what a mess
that wax
caused.

Perhaps this shines
a telling light on the current
state of neurosis: always clawing,
never reaching, on a maddening
spiral staircase to the heavens.
If the observer or its quest
does not shie away from another
layer, herein lays a further ill:
a curious contempt, dare say,
a helpless detestation
for the unremarkable contribution
and the uninspiring wit
a phobia sufficient
to avert the hypothetical
eye, or flee?

In the middle
one is neither
grand nor
simple.

Yet

one must not
delude themselves
with Golidilocks
and the delirious
dilemma
of "just right."

Mosquito Bite

find sorrow's coy note
in heady sanguine liqueur
sip at my story
bijou demise will nourish
invite your kin to the feast

Long Rivers

isolation sought
in a sea of faces found
you rooted me out
i demurred you persisted
repetition wins out

novelty wears quick
my temper is certain death
I implore you leave
your tenacity drowns me
your tenacity saves me

we have built a life
i am the yin to your yang
we have found comfort
on good days it equals joy
other days are bottomless

co-conspirators
we must see this to the end
do not muse over
the subtlety of union
there is no better or worse

In This State

Wind up tick
  toc toes firmly buried in the sand
Look alert smile
  and nod it would not due to not
give a whit bushy
  tailed to the knife edge of plausible
otherwise coast
  fluffy free float oblivion indifference
is no nothing to
  complication or attachment Pin
a pulse to something
  shifting
    fickle
      inconstant
Save the sanity
to mock another day.

It Must Be Nice

wondering
inside the skin
  on this yellow side
of brown
which is darker
in some accounts
and lighter
in others
wondering
about the word
  "elite"
in the same
sentence as
  "freedom"
about causes on
your lapel
and threats

on my life
wondering
how days feel
  breathing
    easy
  mustering
    consternation
yet still living
the exact
  same life
  in the exact
    same world
      as this day
      last week?

It really
must
be nice.

Hotel Jazz

Awash in lethargy
post Jack and Coke daze
my melancholy threatens
atrophy to my limbs
even as its sullied fingers
contract my heart
to insignificance

"Not you,"
that traitorous sax
lows
not your fantasy
to make
keep to your order
and endless lists
day in day out
the monotony
will soon claim you

You ask too much
to be swallowed
by the seduction
to sway in loose limb
abandon
with the siren song
I weave
What you sacrifice to the waters
cannot wash back to you
in the returning waves
Only your sodden
folly and regret.

Pigeons, Not Pedestrians

Sylphs hover in a luminous moment
weightless, impossible vivid
blurs of a cursed treasure
"They must eat like birds!" mused
admiring, bedecked crones.

I craved that adulation,
pronouncements made of me,
ungainly and earthbound, laughable
buffoon. Nature, a mother playing
favourites, each of us not equally
fine, feathered specimens
of avian perfection.

Had we only known better, the old
biddies and this pathetic quack,
our egos preened and fluffed all around:
Every good little birdy worth her salt
eventually caves and eats her body's
weight in insecurity and self-loathing.

Eat or Be Eaten

In crisis
  bellow louder
    than the belligerent
    bovine, screech to
a level, a cacophony,
  a frightening
    simian attack.
        Why
      be so timid
    when words are
      so many bites?
      and tears on pages?
          and action can veer
    towards fatalistic?
The jungle
        dictates that we
          act approrpiately in
            proportion to our
        place in the well-
          worn food
              chain.
      Who says we cannot
          claim our own
            dominance?
        Alpha
    in a fool-
  eats-fool world.

Chat at Your Own Risk

polite conversation
it seems is a bygone past-time
people no longer crave friendship
rather notches on their figurative bedposts
thrills to span the expanse of a thousand heartbeats
shared interests need not find shelter here
that said if your intellect does require
ample tickling and no faltering ego causes a fuss
take a load off you may as well stay awhile

(mothers and daughters and sisters and rants and rambles)

conversation
invariably paired
with coffee
and binging
on life sometimes
food
woes loosened
along with tongues

no alcohol
called for

sister
to sister
a bond across
cultures
and centuries
teased
and tainted

daughter
to mother
the stakes become
higher navigating
the routes becomes
more tricky
they part and twist
and snake
and strike back

we bleed
and no wounds
are apparent
we smile
to bow to pain
would admit
defeat and shame
and acknowledgment
of where
i went wrong
and why you
blame me
and why this sin
is endless, it is endless
in your eyes

there is no
making amends

apologies float on water

my regrets
your shortcomings
become us
not kin to kin
but resentment to rage
and hate
now inextricably forged

my remorse
is in thick suffocating
layers
and i cannot
find the courage
to absolve myself

i pray you can
love yourself
enough
for both of us
and break
this maddening
chain

Role

Mystique trails
an ebony state,
of otherness, of far-
flung lullabies sang
to coarse cotton
hammocks and boiling
crocks of *bigas*

There is a decided
staidness, a reliability,
from mousy
to mahogany, we tilt
our heads up to listen;
nay, heed and digest.
Prudence is best.

Devil may care, steers
with laser purpose,
a hellion flame. Hell hath
no fury, minx, ill-tempered
--perception implodes
when imagination is gifted
free-rein to prance.

When all is laid out
in the sun to dry, the wheat
and the gold trample
every single light. All reverence
and covetous qualms
flattened beneath

we
love you
best.

The Understudy

The beveled gilt
heights and then

One foot elegantly
in
front
of the other
and then

tap

and sudden
leap

swallow
your amazement

curb
your rapid

addiction

this rarified
feat

scoffs
command
performance

answering
merely
to parsimonious
beckoning

audible in conch
shell
shaped ear

Lo!

She ascends
once more
an exquisite
pause

The ground
is ally
or foe

in dizzying
succession

with firm fingers
to guide
forward

do fickle apostles
mourn
an icon
in the presence
of a new muse?

Interject.

I am hearing the jarring thwump-thwump-thwump

of noise inside my head cacophony in three-part

series of I was here and I did this and in my opinion

when--- amidst the whirr-whirr-whirr my voice mollified

nod in agreement nod emphatically nod

> to make
> all sound
> **disappear.**

What Happened to Right?

steeped in outrageous
today, how
in this day and age
enlightenment
has yet to catch up
and human decency
appears on the decline

i have woken up
abruptly
to a harsh alternate
reality, where Superman
is Bizarro, Audrey Hepburn
is a reality television
opportunist and shameless
self-promotion
and vulgarity
are applauded
and admired

where your appearance
excuses your wrongdoing
merits you advantages
culls sympathy

where your appearance
influences quick judgment
courts revilement and fear

gets you killed

i cannot comprehend this
i cannot awaken
from these terrors

i feel i have slumbered
the fitful rest
of Rip Van Winkle
and was reborn
to the death
of all
that is good
and right

V. Musings

Liberty's Womb

Grief cloying, parasitic
in the wake
of our fall from grace, we
prise its vengeful hooks
from comatose form, shame
an idea shaping
with a vertigo efficiency, swept
below consciousness, never
eradicated, only to mingle
with our disgust, our dismay
and disbelief

Nothing we recognise
holds true
Nothing is
as it once had been
We are rendered
children, so frightened
and displaced

Do we now
carry Hatred's Offspring like
death and decay in our belly?
Have we married the void, are we
relegated into this
despotic vacuum, maligned
as societal ills?

We are lost
We are lost

Our despondency
is a wail for a mother to
placate our terror
Nature is parent
and Providence, counsel
a lullaby near
our ear:

Watch the sun
it rises
and sets

Mind the sultry monsoon
faithful to return, time
and time again
a lover's
quivering touch

The world does not
cease, her motions will not
falter

Take comfort,
brethren, see our own
feet, walking forward,
resolute.

First Notions

Thoughts write
themselves into carved
concentric patterns upon
your subconscious pristine
white sheet,

catch up

to commit them, asylum
inhabitants waiting
on initiation to rituals
of further madness or
acolytes, virgin-chaste
to a oracle, to a pyre

burn

those ideas, pick
at them swiftly
while the carrion
wears its blush
mourning garment.

Sway

lubricate my soul
as you souse my ego drunk
stoke my fervor mad.
a mile away if you were
an inch; ever the coquette.

Curd and Whey

Clickety-clack
clique
claque
the egg
before
the chook-chook
the neverending
foolish debate
the fine
line
divisive
among perceived
haves
or have nots
the donkey
the posterior
so different
to some
the same
the deluded
the elite
sometimes
all
the same game

Pecking the Dust for Adoration

This chicken
would fly the musty
coop in the ditsy peacocks
discarded plumage. For, who
wants a sad, dowdy hen?

big sur reveries

oddly, innocent moments
such as these, where the morning
envelopes me in buttercream hush
and my pups are inviting, curled
mochi balls, i am astounded.
the peace is staggering. it
is overwhelming and subtly
addictive. a person can become
swallowed by the virtue that sits
calmly in mystic
santa lucia
syllables.

Showy Birds (aka the "KarJenner Effect")

Puffy crimson
chest and multi-jewel
hued plummage, strut
and mating call to
the most comely peep
no matter that skill
should trump beauty
or sense should dissolve
lust, but does that
matter, topsy-turvy
media-savvy cosm
where visibility
is power and superficial
is the status quo?
Lamented is
the bygone
of grace
in silently
snowy down swans
trampled
in the new
world pecking
order of the insidious
tweet-tweet-tweet.

(tribute to strange fruit)

The unwanted, unknown
is swinging from
the guilty tree limbs
tonight. The magnolias
cloud musty thought
in heady perfume
cloaking
terrible whispered acts
that pierce the silence
once, before flight.

The beautiful
broken ones wait
swinging
in silence
hoping sunlight
finds them first.

labels

labels

a girl is
a girl
black hair
full lip
different
same
borrowed
mine yours

much like
a dog is
a dog-shaped
dog

Tails Out

become lucid
tact
fed to lonesome
minds eager
for taste
of belonging
validation
in conformity
a neat
crevice
where our
neurosis
is neatly
tucked
tails
out

Printed in the United States
By Bookmasters